# *911 ~ Missing Person!*

## *Kate McPhail*

I0133012

*Dragons Wings Publishing*

*Murphy Oregon*

# <u>*911 ~ Missing Person!*</u>

## <u>*Kate McPhail*</u>

Copyright 2017 by Kathryn McPhail

Third Edition

Publisher's Cataloging in Publication Data

McPhail, Kate

911 ~ Missing Person!

1, Young Adult. 2, Adventure. 3, Hiking I Title

Dedicated to Post 18

and

Rick, Sam and Jerry

Special dedication to Jamie who told me I could do

anything if I wanted it bad enough.

Thanks for all the great memories!

# CONTENTS

## ACKNOWLEDGMENTS

Thank you to my friends who have encouraged me to keep writing even when I thought I couldn't!

# 1 MISSING!

My pager rattled, waking me from a sound sleep. I jumped, rolled over and looked at the clock. 4:00 A.M. Bleary-eyed, I checked the number. 555-3214 --the Search and Rescue emergency number-- it must be a search. I grabbed the phone and hit the auto dial, set for Explorer Post 18's emergency response number. A cheerful voice answered, "Good morning! This is Rick."

Biting back my initial reaction to his happiness at this unearthly hour, I mumbled, "'Mornin'. What's up?"

Rick, the leader of one branch of the Marion County Search and Rescue (SAR) Team, said, "We have a missing 12 year old at Breitenbush; can you come?"

Wide-awake now, I asked, "When do I need to report?"

"We need to leave the bus barn at five," he answered.

"Oh, and we may need you to drive," he added. "I'm not sure if Jerry or Ken will make it." They were two more of the advisor team, which also included Rick, Sam and I.

Hanging the phone up, I hurried to prepare. Five o'clock! I thought. That's only 45 minutes from now. I knew the routine; I took the world's fastest shower and dressed in warm wool pants (worn over shorts), a uniform shirt, a waterproof jacket and my hiking boots. I braided my long hair and twisted it into a bun to keep it out of my face.

Hurrying into the kitchen, I grabbed a breakfast bar and took two Lunchables out of the cupboard. Leaving a quick note for my family, who were still blissfully sleeping, I grabbed my always-ready 48-hour pack on the way out the door.

I had forgotten how heavy this thing was! It's been awhile since we had any need for our full packs. In addition to a sleeping bag, these packs consist of all the supplies and food needed for a 48 hour stay 'in the field' if it turned into a long search. Lately, our searches had all been nearby -- close enough to sleep at home. On these searches, we carried only a 24-hour "survival" pack. I opened my car door and tossed my pack into the back seat.

Backing out of the driveway, I felt the familiar pounding of my heart as I shifted my emotions once more into "search mode." I'd been an advisor for Explorer Post 18 for about a year now. We'd had some interesting searches in that time and I wondered if this would be another.

I sped down State Street, which was lightly traveled this early in the morning. My thoughts were jumbled as I drove quickly through the fog. I was glad the traffic was light and happy that I was wearing my uniform; if I were stopped, hopefully, the cop would recognize the "county brown" and give me a break!

As I coasted through a yellow light, I thought about what a busy, eventful season this had been for our rescue team. Four days ago, during water rescue training, Post 18 had a missing person call. We had used our newly trained dive team to pull a drowning victim out of the Willamette River. Then we had just returned yesterday from a two-day search in Polk

County; that one had ended as a suicide. The kids in the Explorer Post were ages 14--21; they were highly trained and professional, but still have had a difficult week! We always had a "debriefing" following any search – especially the difficult ones. This way, any members of the search team could talk through the emotional impact the search made have had.

What was it Rick had said? A twelve-year-old? My heart went out to the parents. Please! I breathed a prayer as I sped to the bus barn. Let this one be O.K. This would be particularly hard for me; I had lost my 13-year-old son, Jason, about three years ago. He had drowned while on a school--sponsored hiking trip. If only a SAR team had been able to find Jason sooner. I still felt guilty, although I was not with him at the time -- I should have been able to save my son. I hated the thought that another mother was hurting for her son.

I shook these thoughts off as I drove into the gravel parking lot, knowing that it was important for me to have my complete focus on this search. As usual, I was one of the first to arrive at the bus barn. The others soon began to arrive, sleepily stomping around in the early morning chill. Sam, another of the advisors, warmed up the huge equipment truck, affectionately known as "Tiny."

I threw my pack in the back and helped as the other search members do the same. One of the other advisors, Jerry, drove in and began to ready the converted bread truck, known as "Baby", as I listed the names of the arriving team members. At 5:10, we were ready to go. Two of the boys climbed into "Tiny" and Sam took the driver's seat. The rest of us would ride in Baby. Jerry offered to drive and I agreed.

## 2 BASE CAMP

As we pulled out onto the road, I called dispatch on the radio to let them know that the Post 18 searchers were on our way to the scene. One group of the more experienced searchers, known as the 'first response team,' had already arrived at the site. They would make a quick preliminary sweep to assess the search area.

Jerry started to give us a quick briefing. "We will be searching for a 12-year-old boy," he began, calmly. "Jon was hiking with his father and a family friend yesterday afternoon, when he apparently wandered off the trail. He has limited hiking experience, is unfamiliar with the area, and is wearing only a tee-shirt, shorts, and tennis shoes."

With a feeling of dread, I thought about this week's weather. During the day, it was a sweltering 95 degrees, but after sundown, in that mountainous area, it was only barely above freezing. Jerry added, "Jon has no food or equipment with him. Also, he is afraid of the dark."

As we hurried to the search site, the van was quiet . . . these kids aren't much older than the missing boy. I thought how hard this must be for them.  My mind raced -- thoughts of Jason intrude as I tried to concentrate on the information about this other mother's son.

Jason had been unprepared, as well; his greatest fear was of water, and he had drowned in rapids, while trying to swim across a river. Once more, I shut off these thoughts as we bumped along in the early morning fog.

In about an hour, we arrived at the small town of Detroit, Oregon. We entered the little restaurant, joining several townspeople, who had already heard about the missing boy. This was where our initial planning would take place; other teams arrived: the horse posse, jeep patrol and a radio relay truck.  Quickly, Jerry was chosen as the search coordinator -- he would be in charge of setting up the search parameters, assigning teams, and calling in other county search teams, if necessary.

I was assigned to be the "runner"-- my duties would include listing the names and units of all the searchers and running messages to and from Jerry. Within a half hour, everyone had their initial assignments and we all headed out to the vehicles to make the drive to the search site.

After a long ride up an extremely narrow, windy and bumpy road, we arrived at the Breitenbush Trail parking lot.  There were only a couple vehicles there: the older pickup that had been driven by the boy's father and a van that had brought the First Response Team up late last night. The rest of our search vehicles were pulled into a roughly semi-circular "camp," which would be our home until the search was over. The members of jeep patrol had already begun a sweep. Their job was to check all roads around the area and form a "fence." If our missing person stumbled onto a road, this team would be able to spot him.

Jerry and Sam, with me trailing along, met with the First Response Team. This was a group of our most experienced kids, who had arrived here last night within a few hours of the missing person's report. They were cheerful, although tired, as they had been up since 4 AM, ready to start searching.

This team had met with the boy's father, who took them up the trail to where Jon was last seen; there, they had found what they believed were shoe prints from his tennis shoes leading off the trail into the brush. They marked the spot, and then headed back to base camp to report to Jerry; they arrived at base camp just a few minutes after we did.

After hearing their report and talking to Jon's father, Mr. Karnac, Jerry set up four teams; there were about 15 kids, not counting the first response team. Each team consisted of a team leader and three or four team members. They were typical teenagers but, during a search, they were truly professionals.

In order to be included in a search, they must have completed 250 hours of training and a first responder First Aid course. Our group had one of the most impressive records in the state for search results. Post 18 searchers usually found what they were looking for. These kids had, over the years, impressed many experienced police officers and other professionals by paying close attention to detail and unselfish willingness to get the job done.

As the teams put on their packs and started up the trail, three more cars arrived. The first car was a Police vehicle; it was a county deputy. He met with Jerry and the rest of the Command Team, in a special area that was being set up under a tent and placed near the radio relay truck. The second car contained Mrs. Karnac and her cousin, who had driven from their home nearly 50 miles south of the popular hiking spot. The third car had a reporter from the local paper. The deputy walked over to the reporter's car and talked with him while we finished setting up base camp.

# 3 THE SEARCH BEGINS

Jerry pulled me aside. "I'd like you to be a liaison to the family. Keep the press away, answer any questions they have, and keep them informed of our progress." With a sympathetic glance at the stricken face of Mrs. Karnac, he added, "Talk to me if they need anything at all."

I walked over and introduced myself to Mrs. Karnac. "I'm Kate; I'm here with the Post 18 search team and will help you in any way I can."

Shocked, pleading eyes look at me. "I...I'm Kathy," she said. Her shoulder-length blond hair hid her eyes as she looked down at her clasped hands.

"Is there anything I can do for you or questions I can answer?" I asked, sympathetically.

Shaking her head, Kathy sat in the chair I had brought over. "I am OK for now," she said. "Just help find my son."

Laying a comforting hand on her shoulder, I nodded. "These searchers are the best," I assure her. "They will do everything they can." She nodded and we sat quietly for a few minutes. Looking up, I saw Mr. Karnac coming toward us. "Here comes your husband, Kathy."

The tall, dark-haired man introduced himself to me, "Hello Kate, I'm Bob." He leaned over and hugged his wife, then sat down beside her. They were silent as they sat side by side, looking somehow as if they did not even know where they were. They both looked numb, as if they couldn't really think beyond the moment they were living in. I knew somewhat how they must be feeling. I remembered how time seemed to stop from the moment I heard those awful words, "your son is missing." I shook my head, willing the memories to go away.

"Let me know if you need anything," I said quietly and went back to Jerry, who was temporarily able to rest. Sam had parked "Tiny" at the base of the trail and joined us.

"Hey, you two want to go for a little walk with me?" Jerry asked. At our nods, he added, "let's go; don't worry about taking anything; we won't go far."

Leaving our packs in camp, we started up the rocky trail. It was a fairly easy hike; at the start, the trail was well defined and had a gentle slope. After about an hour of walking, the trail began to get steeper and more difficult to climb. Sam and I began to realize that we should have brought along our day packs. Luckily, I had a small water bottle attached to my belt; I shared it with my parched partners and we continued our little walk. We had a radio with us, and were keeping in touch with the search teams.

They reported in regularly, as they finished each section. When we had first arrived in base camp, Jerry and Sam had gone over a map of the area and marked it off in a grid pattern. Jerry assigned each team a "square" to search; they would do several sweeps of their assigned area. This way, we could be assured that every area had been covered thoroughly.

The horse posse reported in to let us know they were in Detroit. "Alpha 201 to base." After Jerry's response, we heard, "We have arrived in Detroit. Awaiting search coordinates." Each person in Search and Rescue from our county was assigned "Alpha" numbers -- that was how we identified everyone who participated in a search. Our group was "500," Posse was "200," etc.

Jerry responded, "Hold one, please." We stopped and he spread out the marked map. Only one grid was filled in, so far; the area our first response team had covered early this morning was finished. He radioed, "Base to Alpha 201," and waited for a reply.

"This is Alpha 201," the radio crackled. "Go ahead."

"Alpha 201 start your search along these coordinates," Jerry said. He gave them the map coordinates. I looked over his shoulder to see where he was sending them. This area was too difficult for our ground searchers, but should be easier for the horses. I marveled again at how each group had its own expertise and how smoothly each did their respective jobs.

"10-4, base," the answer came back. "We'll check in when we get there."

Jerry responded, "Copy; Alpha 502 out."

We hiked on for another half hour, until we reached the spot the First Response team had marked. Sam carefully examined the shoe prints. "These look kinda big for a twelve-year-old," he said, doubtfully.

Jerry said, "The father told us that Jon is big for his age. Actually, he's about five-three and weighs about 150 pounds."

Sam nodded. "OK, well, now we know what we are looking for. Did the parents identify these?"

Jerry nodded. "The mother told us what kind of shoes he was wearing," he stated. He added, "We called the description into headquarters and they faxed us these pictures of the treads." He showed the pictures to Sam and they compared them to the smudged prints.

Again, I was fascinated at the technology Post 18 had access to. I always was impressed by how thorough our searches were; we used every resource possible to find missing people. Post 18 was also called in often to assist the police in searching for crime evidence--we had an almost 100 percent "find" rate for weapons and other evidence.

# 4 NO SIGN OF JON

We headed back to base camp. It didn't take quite as long to get back down the trail. On the way back down the trail, Sam and I teased Jerry about his "little walk!" We had used all my water, so hurried to the fountain in the parking lot as soon as we reached camp. Sam and I had a quick discussion as Jerry slurped his water down; we decided to carry our packs the next time Jerry suggested a walk.

"Alpha 701 to base." The radio crackled. 700 was the Alpha number assigned to another one of the support groups. This one was a small group called Radio Emergency Action Citizen Team, or REACT. They were responsible for monitoring radio emergency calls and calling the proper agencies to assist stranded motorists, accident victims, etc. They also provided food for Post 18's trainings and searches.

Jerry answered, "Base. Go ahead, 701." He turned to us and added, "Looks like Don made it."

"I am in Detroit. What is the road like up to base camp?"

"701, it is steep and rocky. Our maps said it is an 'unimproved' road. They were right!"

Don's voice crackled through the radio. "Do you think I can make it up there?"

Jerry hesitated and looked at us. Sam and I shook our heads doubtfully. "We need food for later, but... I don't think your van would make it."

"Copy, base," the radio crackled again. "What would you like me to do?"

Sam and Jerry conferred briefly. Jerry said, "Base to 701. We are setting up tonight at the high school there in town. They had arranged for us to shower and sleep there if we need to. Why don't you set up a canteen there?"

"10-4. I'll check in tonight again when the chili is hot. Alpha 701 out."

"Base out."

Jerry turned to me. "Why don't you check to see how the family's holding up?"

I nodded and walked over to the car, where Bob and Kathy were sitting with Kathy's cousin. As I got closer, I heard the cousin saying in a loud, whiney voice, "I don't get it! Why don't they call out more people? They are just sitting around. Look at them!" She pointed to a group of kids sitting in the sun.

I walked up and said, "I think that's the team who just came back after searching all night."

Bob nodded. "Yes, it is." He added, "They met me at the top late last night and spent the rest of the night searching all the way along the trail."

"Oh," said the cousin. "But why haven't they called someone else to hunt for poor Jonny? When are they going to start looking again?"

Patiently, I explained that we had several teams in the area searching. "We have several ground teams, a jeep patrol, and a horse posse right now," I told her. "If we don't find him right away, we have put several other teams on call."

"Well, I haven't seen any other teams," she said. "And poor, poor Jonny! He's probably so scared!" She wandered off towards the radio and Jerry.

Watching her leave, I shook my head and turned to Kathy. "Is there anything I can do for you?" I asked.

She looked at her cousin, who was talking and gesturing wildly to Jerry. "Can you keep her away from me?" she asked. "She is driving me nuts!"

"I'll see what I can do," I said. "Anything else?"

"Not right now," she said. Her eyes were bloodshot and had dark circles under them. I patted her shoulder and assured her that I would continue to keep her informed as soon as there was any news and she nodded, wearily.

Bob asked me to take a walk with him. I agreed and we walked a little way down the road. "Is there any news at all yet?" he asked me.

I shook my head. "Not yet," I said. "But, many of our teams have just begun their second or third sweeps; they'll do everything they can, Bob. I promise you that."

"I know," he said. "I am really impressed with their professionalism and their concern. They seem to really care."

"They do," I assured him. "How is your wife holding up?"

He slowly shook his head. "Not so well," he said. "I'm sending her home when I can convince her to go; she can't do anything here and our daughter needs her."

"That's probably a good idea," I said. "She will still worry, but it would be easier for her if she concentrates on keeping the others calm." I knew what I was talking about. Through the long week before Jason's body was found, the needs of my other children kept me focused. I didn't share that thought with Bob.

# 5 WAITING

We continued walking quietly for a few minutes, and then looked up as a car drove into the parking lot. Bob said, "That's my brother-in-law. Come on over and I'll introduce you."

We walked over to the car and I was introduced to Mike, a soft-spoken blond man about 25 years old. Bob said, "I'm going back to sit with Kathy for a while." Mike and I walked back towards the radio van, where I introduced him to Jerry. He told us that he wanted to help, so Jerry suggested that I take him over to the team getting ready to head out again. I introduced Mike to Susan, the team leader. "Jerry suggested that Mike go with your team," I told Susan.

"OK. Do you have any equipment?" Susan asked.

Nodding, Mike indicated a large fanny pack with an attached water canteen. Susan assigned a team member to hike next to Mike, in case he had questions or needed assistance. Post 18 doesn't usually allow family members to go with a team, but Mike appeared calm and was willing to listen to the team leader. He thanked me and followed the team as they headed back up the trail, discussing strategy.

I returned to Jerry and told him about Kathy's request to keep the cousin away from her. He smiled sympathetically. "I've met her." He nodded towards the deputy, who was visibly struggling to stay patient as the woman nattered away. Jerry pondered for a moment. "I know," he said. "I'll send her down to help Don -- he'll need some help getting a hot meal ready for this evening!" Sam and I nodded. That way, she would be out of our hair and Don wouldn't need to ask one of the kids to help.

Jerry sent me over to tell her our idea; she smiled, pleased to have an important job, and the deputy agreed to take her down to Detroit. He rolled his eyes at Jerry as they left. Jerry sent him a salute.

I returned to Kathy and told her that we found a job for her cousin. She smiled in relief and asked, "Would you mind sitting here with me for awhile?" I sat down and listened as she shared all her fears for her son. Bob had gone for another walk along the road; Kathy told me that was his outlet for stress.

The long day passed slowly. Every time the radio crackled, everyone in camp stopped what they were doing and listened intently. However, every report was about the same. "Team three to base."

"This is base; go ahead team three."

"Base, we have finished our sweep and are ready to begin the next sweep."

"Base copies. Continue team three.  Base out."

"10-4; team three out"

Jerry, Sam, and the others on the command team would check the map and mark off each grid that had already been searched. Occasionally, a car would pull into the parking lot and several people in hiking gear would approach the camp. Everyone who asked was given a description of Jon and a dedicated number to call if he was seen.

It began to get dark. Kathy was finally convinced to go home. She said she would stop to pick up her cousin and would keep in touch. She hugged me as she left, looking exhausted, but still trying to be hopeful. Bob decided to remain in camp with Mike, who had returned with Susan's team, tired but happy that he was able to help. I had been with the family most of the day; listening when they needed to talk and answering many questions about our training and experiences with search and rescue.

At nine PM, we called off the search for the night as the last team reported back to base.  I invited Bob and Mike to stay with us in Detroit at the High school, but hey decided to sleep in their cars. Bob told me, "I want to be here if Jonny finds his way back to the parking lot."

"I understand," I told him. "Is there anything I can get for you while I'm in town?"

Bob shook his head, but Mike asked me to pick up a razor and call his wife. "Let her know that I'm staying up here," he said. "... and that I love her," he added with a touch of embarrassment. He had told me earlier that they had just been married last month. I smiled and took the $5 and paper he had written his phone number on.

I climbed back into the bread truck along with 10 tired and hungry searchers. On the long trip back down the windy, bumpy road, we all discussed the day's search. Jerry told us that Rick was in Detroit and we would have our debriefing while we ate some hot chili that Don had prepared for us. At the news of dinner, the tired and hungry kids all cheered. Laughingly, I teased them, "you must really like Rick a lot!" They laughed back and soon settled down to doze until we reached Detroit.

When we reached the school, we found Don's van set up and the smell of food wafting towards us. Everyone hurried over to grab a handful of crackers, some fruit and a big bowl of steaming hot chili.

# 6 A NIGHT'S REST

They all settled down to serious munching as I went into the store to buy the razor and made Mike's phone call. I was smiling as I came out of the store and went to pick up a bowl of chili. Rick came over to talk to me.

"How are you doing?" he asked.

"I'm OK," I told him, wondering why he asked.

"Well, Jamie, Jerry and I are a little concerned about you and this particular search," he said.

Understanding dawned on me. These three were the only members of the search group who knew about Jason and how he had died.

Rick added, sympathetically, "We are worried about how you will deal with it if things do not turn out well."

I thought about it for a minute. "I think I'll be OK," I said. "I've talked to the parents a lot today, and I can empathize with how they are feeling."

Rick nodded. "They both told Jerry how grateful they are for your support. Just let us know if it gets to be too hard for you."

I nodded my head. "Thanks, but I think I'll be fine." I knew that this search was important for me. I felt as if I was helping Jason somehow -- like I hadn't been able to do before. I told Rick some of this, and he nodded in understanding.

Laying his hand on my shoulder, he said again, "Well, just let us know if it begins to be too difficult." He smiled at me and went to confer with Jerry. I moved over to sit by Jamie and Sara who were here from their posts at the main Sheriff's office. They were graduates of the program and were "junior advisors" until age 21.

I had a lot of respect for them; they had both been members since they were 14 and had been on a lot of searches. They had taught me a lot about what teenagers were capable of and had restored my faith in the future. We chatted quietly for awhile until Rick and Jerry joined us. "I wonder if you would mind doing me a favor, Kate," Rick began.

I nodded. "Sure, what do you need?" I asked.

Rick looked over to where the searchers were sprawled out eating and joking to relieve their stress. "Some of these kids need to go home," he told me. "Most of them haven't had any sleep since the Polk county search. I'm afraid they will get burned out."

I answered, "Yes, I noticed that a few are a little 'slap happy' tonight. Sure, I'll take them home. Do you want me to return tonight?"

Rick shook his head. "No, just wait until morning. I've called out a few more searchers. You can bring them up in the morning. I told them to report to the bus barn at 0500."

We started over to the van and he handed me the keys. "You sure you are OK?" he asked quietly.

I knew he was still worried that there might be some bad memories surfacing. I nodded. "Yes, I'm OK. Thanks, though."

"Well," he added. "If you need to talk..." He trailed off.

I nodded. "I know." Changing the subject, I asked, "Which kids are going back?"

Rick told me he would round them up for me. I went over and 'fired up' the van. Several sleepy teens soon joined me. Rick gave me a list of the kids which I would be bringing back in the morning.

I nodded and pulled out of the parking lot. The trip home was long and quiet as only one of the kids stayed awake. She and I talked softly about life in general as I drove. When we arrived at the bus barn, the kids climbed stiffly out and got into their cars. "Drive carefully," I said, feeling like a mother hen. They all gave me a nod and a wave as they drove away.

It was midnight. I had called my family earlier, so I decided to sleep in "Baby." It was NOT the most restful night I have ever had!

5 AM sure comes early, I thought as I stumbled out of the van and tried to walk out the stiffness. A couple cars drove into the parking lot, and five sleepy teens tumbled out with their packs. Throwing their stuff in the back of "Baby," they signed the roster and climbed into the van. I pulled out of the parking lot and called Jerry on the radio. "512 to base."

A sleepy voice answered. "This is base, go ahead, 512."

"I'm on my way back to base camp."

"Copy, 512. See you in an hour."

I drove through the foggy morning, back up the mountain. I hoped we would find Jon today. I wondered how cold it had been last night -- he was only wearing shorts and a tee shirt. A picture flashed into my mind; Jason stood, smiling at me, wearing his favorite purple flowered shorts. I smiled through suddenly misty eyes. I didn't like those shorts, but he had bought them with his own money and was so proud the day he had brought them home. They were the ones he was wearing when -- I stopped that thought and forced my mind back to the search.

I had seen Jon's picture yesterday and talked with his parents many times; I felt like I knew him. I breathed a quick prayer for his safety as we arrived at the Detroit school.

"Welcome home." Jamie greeted me cheerfully as I stiffly climbed out of the van. "Sleep well?"

"Sure," I lied. "I always sleep well in a cramped position in a cold van next to a busy fire station!"

He laughed as Jerry and Sam came over to the van. Jerry asked, "You want to drive back up to base?"

Shaking my head, I slid over and gestured for him to take the wheel. He rounded up the rest of the team as Sam climbed into the van, joining the half-awake group in the back. In five minutes we were on our way to the base camp again.

We drove back up the winding, bumpy road -- it seemed worse today. Arriving in camp, we pulled up behind Bob and Mike who were awake and eating apples for breakfast. I handed Mike his razor and told him his wife sent her love. He blushed and nodded his thanks. Kathy had decided to stay home, Bob told me.

He assured me that he was doing fine. I took a walk up the road with Mike to see what he thought. He said, "Bob is holding up well. He's a strong guy -- he'll be OK."

I asked, "How about Kathy?"

Mike shook his head. "She's doing great so far," he said. "I don't know how she'll react if..." he trailed off.

"Well," I said, reassuringly. "We are doing everything possible to find Jon." He nodded and headed back to Bob, who was talking with Rick and Sam.

# 7 DAY TWO

I stopped to refill my canteen and then went over to Jerry to ask him what he would need me to do today. He told me to stay with the family. A few more people had arrived and he pointed out a large motor home and told me it was for them to use if they needed a quiet place to rest.

There were several other units arriving from neighboring counties; Jerry asked me to get a list of all members of each unit. I drifted from unit to unit collecting more and more names. Each unit had a different specialty.

There was a canine unit from one county, some trackers from Warm Springs Indian Reservation, climbers, another horse posse, a radio van and two more Explorer Posts. The county Sheriff's office had sent up a couple deputies, one to assist in coordinating the search and another to handle the PR. Because this was a missing child, it had become big news and more media began to arrive. Two news vans and several private cars drove in and parked near the trail head. Reporters and cameramen began asking questions of the searchers and looking around for the family. There were now more than 100 people milling around in our base camp area, which had already been a little crowded yesterday.

The search helicopter, on loan to us from the National Guard, reported in. The radio kept crackling, as more units reported in when they finished their sweeps. Jerry was in the middle of a briefing as I took a walk over to see what needed to be done.

"Hey, Kate, could we have some coffee here?" Jerry looked up briefly and smiled as I nodded and turned to see what I could round up. The Red Cross had set up a food van, so I asked the man there about coffee.

He said, "Comin' up as soon as possible. You want some soup or a sandwich?"

My stomach rumbled. I looked at my watch and realized it had been several hours since last night's chili. Smiling, I asked, "What kind of sandwiches do you have?"

He allowed me to choose from a variety of deli meats and I made a sandwich and ate as he finished making a big pot of coffee. I took it and a stack of Styrofoam cups over to Jerry's table. The serious-faced people there gratefully reached out and poured steaming cups of coffee.

Words drifted towards me from the group, "What would an inexperienced kid be most likely to do?  Go up or down?"  My training had taught me that it was important to spend some time trying to imagine where the missing person would probably go. The hard part was that kids usually got scared and did the opposite of what an adult would. Jon's inexperience and age made it harder to predict what he might do.

Today's search was much like the day before, but there was an added sense of urgency.  We knew that time was running out for Jon.  He wouldn't be able to last much longer without food.  Plus the nights were cold and no one knew if he would know how to stay warm.  The long day passed with no good news.  I spent most of it replenishing the coffee pot and sitting with Mike and Bob.   Sometimes we talked a little; mostly, we just sat and hoped and waited and prayed.

There was a mountain climber group and one of our teams still in the field as the sun went down.  They called in to report their locations. The climbers reported that they would stay where they are until morning. Jerry asked our team, "How long would it take you to get to base?"

The group leader answered, "About two hours."

"10-4," Jerry said. "Then you might as well stay there. It will save you time tomorrow, too."

"10-4, Base!" came the excited reply. These kids had the training, equipment and experience to spend the night out. In fact, they actually liked to sleep on the ground! I was glad I could sleep inside where it would be warmer.

We climbed into the van and headed down to the grade school. I was glad that I would not have to sleep on the lumpy front seat of the van tonight.

On the way back down the mountain, we listened to the news on the radio. Suddenly, everyone sat up straight as we heard a surprising announcement... "According to a source at the search scene, Jon Karnac, the twelve year old boy who disappeared while hiking in the Breightenbush Wilderness area, was found about an hour ago. There are no details about his condition at this time . . ."

There was a stunned silence in the van. Then pandemonium broke out.

"What?" Jerry said in a shocked tone.

"Who found him?" I asked, speaking to no one in particular.

Everyone began talking at once. We were trying to make sense of this very strange news report. Jerry called for quiet, and we all looked at him, hoping for an answer. Jerry said, "I'm going to call and see if I can find out what is happening."

We pulled off to the side of the road and waited, listening as Jerry called Rick at the main dispatch center, trying to get more information. "Alpha 501, this is Alpha 502," he said. When the radio crackled an answer, he continued. "Did you hear the news report? What's going on?"

Rick's voice came through the static. "I heard. I'm still trying to track down who found him! And why this is the first time we are hearing it . . . ?"

The van was silent as we waited for a few tense minutes. Rick came back on the radio. "The news anchor checked and said it was a 'mistake'. Jon is still missing! Someone claiming to be from the media called the station and made the report, but no one is admitting to it."

Jerry asked, "Why did they report it without confirmation from us?"

Rick replied, "That is what I asked and they said it apparently came from a trusted source!" He added, "I am going to call Mrs. Karnac and make sure she didn't hear this. What an awful thing to do. I hope they can quickly figure out who told them and I also hope the punishment is serious!"

# 8 "WE SEE A BODY"

We drove on; discussing this development and wondering at the cruelty which would make someone give a false report like that. I was surprised at how angry these kids were, but then remembered how dedicated they were and how hard they had been working searching for Jon.

We finally reached the school, where there were rows of cots set up in the gymnasium. After a quick meal provided by REACT, I fell into bed. The sounds of teens laughing and letting off steam faded as I drifted into an uneasy sleep, troubled by vague dreams of Jason calling for help.

Early the next morning, we set off for base camp. As we bumped along up the narrow road, the kids slowly began to wake up and talked among themselves quietly. I asked Jerry, "How long do you think we will keep searching?"

"Just between us," he answered, "Today will be our last day."

I looked at him in shock. "Why today?" I asked.

He glanced into the mirror to make sure the kids were not listening to our conversation. "Well, we usually don't search more than two days," he said. "Today is the third day with no sign. Jon's chances are not looking too good. We will probably pull most of the teams out today at noon." He sighed, "This is a frustrating search. I wish we could find SOME sign of which way he went! How are the parents holding up?"

I answered, "They are doing OK. Kathy is trying hard to stay hopeful. Bob is keeping her spirits up fairly well."

He glanced at me. ". . . and you? How are you doing?"

I gulped. "It is difficult . . . but I am doing OK. I am concentrating on helping Bob and Kathy."

He smiled sympathetically. "Just let us know if you need to go home," he said. "No one would blame you."

I nodded. We had arrived at Base Camp. Everyone crawled out and quietly joined their assigned teams. The mood this morning was grim. Everyone seemed to sense that time was running out for Jon.

Base camp was even fuller than before; more searchers had arrived from neighboring counties. Everyone was milling around waiting for Jerry to tell them where to start searching.  He sat down at the "command" table and talked with the group leaders as they drifted over to consult with him.  I talked with each group and started another roster with the names of the new groups and how many searchers were with them.

As the command group began planning strategy and how to best utilize the new resources, I walked over to Bob.  He introduced me to the people with him.  His father had arrived, along with several neighbors and relatives.  He looked exhausted as he explained who I was and how much help I had been.  Embarrassed, I blushed.  Bob's dad asked me, "Is there any news?"

Before I could answer, the radio nearby crackled to life.  An excited voice said, "Tracker team 1 to base.  Subject has been located! We are requesting rescue helicopter to this location.  Repeat--subject has been located!"

The entire camp went suddenly silent.  Everyone seemed to be holding their breath.  There was a sudden intake of breath, as everyone suddenly realized what they had just heard.

Hurrying over to the radio, I waited and listened for the helicopter to report in.

Finally, we hear, "Air 1 to base."

Jerry said, "Come in Air 1."

"Arriving at coordinates. We can see a body lying on the ground, covered with a blanket."

My heart dropped. Covered body? NO! Please, let him be alive!

# 9 IN THE HELICOPTER

I glanced at Jerry, who frantically signaled towards the large motor home next to where we were standing. I nodded at him and turned to Bob. As the news crews began hurrying towards us, I quietly suggested that we go inside the motor home. The entire group turned without a word and walked over to the motor home. The news reporters began hurrying towards us, as I closed the door. One of the Command Crew stepped towards them.

"Let's wait in here," I said, as calmly as I could manage. Numbly, the group sat looking at me with anxious eyes. The news crews stopped and began to mill around outside the door, but walked back towards the radios when they saw that we were staying inside.

For a moment, no one said anything. Then Mike asked, "What's going on? Is Jon OK?"

"I don't know," I answered. "Let me go see what I can find out." I looked at Bob, who was fighting to stay calm. Looking him in the eyes, I said quietly, "I promise to tell you as soon as I know anything at all." He nodded and sighed deeply, as if he had been holding his breath. I looked around at the friends and relatives and said a little louder, "I will be back as soon as I find out what is happening."

I stepped out of the motor home. The crowd was milling around the command tent. There was little conversation, as everyone seemed to be frozen, waiting for news. The camp stayed silent as we all held our breaths and waited for the helicopter crew to make its next report. I glanced towards the motor home, hoping they were far enough away to be unable to hear the radio, which seemed abnormally loud in the silence.

Everyone in the motor home was looking down. I wondered if they were praying. I whispered a silent prayer of my own as the radio burst back to life.

"Air 1 to Base. Subject is alive. He is hungry and wants to go home. Repeat . . ." The rest was drowned out by the excited murmurs of the searchers and newsmen crowded around the radio. I spun around, twisting my ankle on a rock as I hurried to the motor home. Opening the door and looking directly into Bob's hope-filled eyes, I blurted, "He's alive -- and OK!"

Everyone burst into tears. Bob stood up, shaking, as I hugged him. He began to sob. The door opened and Jerry stepped in with an ear-to-ear smile. The media was clamoring outside the door. Bob pumped Jerry's hand wordlessly, as I gave and received hugs from most of the others in the motor home. Jerry, a little choked, said, "The helicopter is on its way back to camp with Jon. Would you like to meet it?" Bob, tears still running down his face, grabbed my arm for support and started towards the door.

Jerry reached the door first and asked the media and the others to back away. The crowd stepped back respectfully, although many of them reached out to touch Bob as he and I slowly followed Jerry through the crowd. As we saw the helicopter landing at the other side of the parking lot, the news crews began surging forward. The Command Group and I stood between the crowd and Bob as a group of National Guard members came into sight, walking with a scratched, dirty young boy.

He had a huge smile on his tear-streaked face, which widened as he saw his dad waiting. He broke into a stumbling run — straight into his father's arms. They stood wrapped in happiness and relief as the rest of us smiled through our tears.

When Bob was finally able to let go, several other people hugged Jon as we made our way back to the motor home. Several people brought fruit and other food to the door and Jon was fed until he couldn't force another bite. I began cleaning his wounds as he told his family about the last three nights. He told us he stayed near the river and ate berries, as he tried to find a campground. I saw the news people frantically trying to hear every word.

Jon looked as his dad and said, "I remembered which ones were poison and didn't eat them, Dad!"

Bob smiled and told us, "We had talked about which berries were good for eating."

Jon continued his story. He was interrupted several times by well-wishers offering him more food and mementos. The leader of the dog team came over and handed him a tee-shirt. Jon told him, "I heard the dogs barking one night and hoped they would hurry up and find me!"

The dog team leader shook his head. "Our dogs are trained NOT to bark," he said. "They need to be quiet so we can listen."

Jon looked puzzled. He said, "But, I know I heard dogs barking."

Bob said, "You probably heard wolves."

Jon eyes widened. "T-there are wolves out there?" Everyone smiled at the expression on his face.

He shrugged and said, "Well, I did see some other animals out there. That's why I carried this." He held up a thick tree branch, which we had carried from the helicopter. At the puzzled looks, he added, "it was to hit the bears with if they came after me!"

Everyone laughed and Jon looked down in embarrassment. I whispered, "I would have done the same thing!" He grinned at me.

Jerry signaled me and I went over to where he was standing in the doorway. "Sara is here and will finish the first aid. Would you like to ride in the helicopter?"

"Would I ever!" I said with a smile.

As we walked towards the helicopter, he noticed that I was limping badly. "What's wrong with your leg?" he asked in concern.

I shrugged. "I twisted my leg when I was running to tell Bob that Jon was OK," I said. "It hurts more now that it did at first."

He said, "Be sure to have it looked at." At my nod, he continued. "The helicopter pilot asked if anyone from base camp would like to see the search area." Not looking at me, he added. "I thought you deserved a reward for all your hard work."

I was unsure how to respond. "Thank you," I mumbled.

He nodded as we arrived at the landing site. I was introduced to the flight crew and we climbed into the helicopter. I was nervous, since I had never ridden in a 'copter' before. As I realized there were no seats or doors, I became even more nervous! The crew explained that we would sit on boxes, which were tied to the floor. They helped me fasten a seatbelt, which was a 4 inch wide strap bolted to the floor. One of the crew helped me wrap it around my waist and cinched it tight. "Don't worry," the pilot smiled. "We haven't lost very many civilians — yet!" I smiled shakily. Jerry was sitting next to me; he looked a little nervous, too, which helped.

The engine began to whine -- louder and louder. Then, suddenly, we were off the ground. Within a short time, we were flying just above the trees. The pilot took us over the entire search area, showing us all the areas which had been searched. He ended our roar by showing us where Jon had finally been located. As I looked at the rugged terrain, I realized why it had taken the searchers such a long time to find Jon.

Then, too soon, we were back on the ground. I hobbled back to the van, which was filled with tired, but jubilant teens, ready to go home.

This time the drive down the mountain was more relaxed as the happy teens began letting off steam. These kids had worked hard and Jerry and I smiled at their silliness. The trip home took about two hours, but seemed longer, because sitting made my leg hurt more. By the time we arrived back at the parking lot, my leg was throbbing with pain.

Rick met the van and watched my pain-filled exit; he advised me to go straight to the doctor. "Our group is covered by workman's compensation insurance," he told me. I nodded. He handed me a paper with the insurance numbers and then handed me his cell phone. "Call someone to pick you up, so you don't have to drive yourself home," he advised.

"No problem," I tried to smile. "My husband came to pick up the car yesterday." I called home and he arrived about 15 minutes later.

We drove directly to the hospital, where there was the usual long wait in the waiting room. While I was waiting to see a doctor, several people noticed my uniform (still recognizable under the dirt) and asked me about the search. Everyone expressed relief that Jon was OK.

I answered several questions about Post 18 and even took down a name and number from a teenager with a broken arm who was interested in more information about joining the Post.

I finally saw a doctor, who x-rayed, poked and prodded, then decided I had pulled the large muscle beside the knee.  He gave me some pain pills, and advised me to stay off the leg for a week.  We left, stopping by the pharmacy on the way home, where I picked up a pair of crutches and then went home to sleep for several hours.

# 10 AFTERWARDS

The following day, I was surprised to receive a phone call from Mike! He was calling to invite me (and my family) to a "welcome home" party for Jon. I tried to explain that it sounded like a family thing, but he told me Bob had specifically asked me to be there. "After all," he added, "You are family now. And we would like to thank you for all your hard work."

Although I was embarrassed, I agreed and he gave me directions to the house. We arrived in the small town where Jon lived and saw a huge "Welcome Home, Jon!" sign on the front porch. Several people were milling around in the front yard. As I got out of my car, I saw Jon standing on the porch waiting for me. He was cleaner than when I had seen him last, but I was shocked at the angry red scratches still visible on his face, arms and legs. He noticed my wince and grinned. "It doesn't feel as bad as it looks," he said.

I smiled as I used my crutches to hobble across the yard. As I reached the porch, Jon wrapped me in a bear hug. "I didn't get a chance to thank you yesterday," he said.

I murmured, "I didn't really do anything special."

"My mom and dad told me how nice you were to them," he said. Suddenly becoming aware of my crutches, he asked, "What happened to you? Were you on crutches yesterday?"

Red-faced, I replied, "No. I was so excited to tell your Dad you were found, that I stepped on a rock and twisted my knee."

There was a sudden flash. Startled, I realized a photographer had just taken our picture. The man smiled at me and said," hey, that would make a GREAT story! Would you be willing to talk to one of our reporters?"

Turning a deeper red, I stammered, "I-I guess so."

He pointed to a woman sitting across the yard. "When she finishes talking to those people, I know she will want to talk to you."

I nodded, and then escaped into the house. Bob and Kathy both hugged me and introduced me to several of their friends and neighbors. "Kate helped a lot," Bob told them. "She was a great listener and helped us stay sane."

Several people asked me about Search and Rescue; I told them it was a volunteer organization made up of several units. When I described the training and how impressive the kids were, Bob added, "That's true! They are very professional and thorough."

After talking for awhile and eating some great barbecued chicken, I returned outside to talk to the reporter. She asked me many questions about Post 18. Then she asked more about the search for Jon.

"It was a long and frustrating search," I told her. "But, luckily, this one had a happy ending."

The reporter asked me to talk about how I had gotten involved in Search and Rescue. I asked her NOT to print that part of my story; after she agreed, I told her about my son, Jason.

The following day, a friend of mine sent over six copies of the paper. My picture and a long article about the search were on the front page!

I have never forgotten that long ago search. It was a turning point in my life. Although there would be many other searches -- with good endings and bad -- I knew that no other would ever be so personal to me.

I felt that my son's memory could now rest in peace, for I had played a small part in restoring the son of another mother, sparing her the pain, the anger and the helplessness of loss.

# APPENDIX I

# STANDARD SEARCH AND SURVIVAL EQUIPMENT

This list, developed by the Seattle Mountaineers, was made up to give to people who asked what they should take to go hiking.  It is the MINIMUM that anyone should take with them on any outdoor activity.   The TEN ESSENTIALS are:

1       Whistle

2       Extra food and clothing

3       sun glasses

4       Compass

5       Flashlight, extra bulb and batteries

6       Map of the area

7       Knife

8       Matches in a waterproof container

9       Fire Starters

10      First Aid Kit

Required by POST 18

Wear on your body:

A heavy duty Pocket Knife (recommend 3-5"folding knife with locking blade)

A compass

A watch

A whistle

We always had two packs.  One was our "24 hour" pack, which is a basic "search and survival" pack required on all searches.  This was a small back pack or fanny pack, filled with various "kits." The kits consisted of small bags filled with essentials. The second pack was our "48-hour" pack, which was a frame pack including extra items we would need if the search lasted longer than a day.

Included in a 24-hour pack:

1)      Small flashlight

2)      quart-size water bottle

3)       10' x 12' tarp

4)      Heavy leather gloves

5)      Folding saw

6)      50-100 feet of twine

7)      Sunglasses

8)      Surveyor's flagging tape

9)      Personal comfort kit (I put these items in a quart size zip lock bag)

            Toilet paper, in zip lock bag (so it stays dry)

            Insect repellant

            Sun screen (highest SPF available)

            Chap Stick

            Small bar of soap, in zip lock bag

            Several paper towels, in zip lock bag

            Anything else you may need (toothpaste, brush, etc)

10)     First aid kit (These items also fit into a quart size zip lock bag)

    Four 4" X 4" sterile gauze pads

    Twelve Band-Aids

    Five aspirin or Tylenol tablets

    Three Tums or other antacids

    One triangular bandage

    Package of Gatorade

    Roll of 1 or 2 inch wide roller gauze (Kling)

    Tube of antiseptic

    Personal medications

    Small roll of adhesive tape (waterproof)

    Rubber gloves

    You may want to add other things, such as scissors, moleskin, tweezers, a snakebite kit, etc. Keep in mind that everything you add makes the kit (and your pack) heavier.


11)     Survival kit      (Again, a quart size bag works well)

    Water purification (tablets, chlorine, etc)

    Twenty-four matches in a waterproof container

    Three fire starters (candle stubs, fire ribbon, etc.)

    1 spare compass (5 degree increments)

Cell phone (for emergency phone calls)

Spare knife

Scratch paper and pencil

5 sugar cubes in zip lock bag

Instant tea, coffee or chocolate

Two packets of instant soup

Medium size plastic garbage bag


12) Repair kit (This kit fits into a sandwich or snack size bag)
Needle

Small bobbin of thread

Two safety pins

Extra boot lace

12" piece of bailing wire

Spare flashlight batteries and bulbs

Small roll of tape


48-hour pack: Besides the items listed above, our 48 hour pack included:

1) Sleeping bag

2) ground cloth or foam insulating pad

3) Rain jacket and pants

4)      Change of underwear and socks (a zip lock bag will help keep them dry and will work as a dirty/wet clothes bag)

5)      Lightweight wool sweater

6)      Pair of wool pants

7)      Enough food for one meal (freeze dried or MRE)

8)      Garbage bag (I put mine over my sleeping bag)


After the initial training period, we were also allowed to carry a backpacking stove and a tent in our packs.

Other hints:

Recommended is a supply of "nibble food" in a zip lock bag.

Be prepared for ANY kind of weather.

Label everything in your pack with your name.

Restock your pack after every outing.  That way, you will always be prepared.  I added a typed list of contents to each kit, in order to help me check for needed supplies.

# APPENDIX II

FIRE MAKING

Besides matches, you may want to have a flint.  By shaving it with your pocket knife to make a spark on a pile of fire starter, this method can start a fire.  If you are truly "outdoorsy" you may want to try using an old Native American method to make your fire.  This technique is called the bow drill method.

MATERIALS:

Most of the materials you need can be easily found in the woods.  Once you have made a bow drill, you can add it to your pack, if you want.  I suggest taking waterproof matches with you, however, as this method takes some practice.

1) Wood — cottonwood, sagebrush or white elm

2) Green curved stick, 24" long, with a fork on one end for the bow

3) Leather cord, 30" long, with a split in one end; small plug

4) Stone or hardwood spindle handle (should fit in your palm)

5) Shredded bark of cottonwood, birch, cedar or sage for tinder

6) Bark slab to catch the spark

7) Spindle, 6" to 8" long, pointed at one end (made of yucca, cottonwood or white elm)

8) Wooden board — cut a dip into board for spindle

INSTRUCTIONS:

Tie cord to unsplit end of bow, slip plug into split and twist the cord.

Slip plug end into the forked end of bow.

Put slotted board over the bark slab. Set your left foot on the board to the left of the hole.

Insert spindle bottom between cord and bow, then twist it so the cord goes around the spindle once.

Brace left arm around knee with spindle handle in left hand. Insert spindle in handle and board.

With the right hand draw the bow back and forth gradually increasing pressure with left hand. Keep pumping with right hand until smoke appears at bottom of board.

Take the coal and gently dump it into the tinder; blow lightly until the bark ignites Make sure you have enough small kindling to keep the fire going.

From *Native American Crafts and Skills* by David Montgomery.

# APPENDIX THREE

# General Information on Search and Rescue

The sheriff is in charge of Search and Rescue for his county. His job is to provide leadership, co-ordinate the resources, provide information to the press and make the final decision on when to end the search. If the search is on National or State Forest land, forest rangers work with the sheriff.

In Oregon, the State Sheriff's Association sets the minimum training standards for search teams and sponsors statewide training classes. Each search team also may add their own specialized training.

The Oregon State Department of Emergency Management is the information center for the state's Sheriff's offices. They may call other — outside the area — units if it is necessary.

# Types of Search Teams

In most of the United States, Search and Rescue is done by volunteers working under command and coordination of the Sheriff. Units which can be called in for a search and rescue mission include: National Guard helicopters or communication units; Civil Air Patrol airplanes; mountain rescue teams; amateur radio operators (such as Radio Emergency Action Citizen Team -- REACT); Red Cross; snow mobiles; horse rescue groups; 4-wheel drive units (jeep patrol) and ground units, such as search dog units, trackers and Explorer groups like Post 18.

Each unit specializes in certain types of searches and may not be needed for every missing person or other search. Some teams may also provide assistance during trainings. For example, in Marion County (Oregon), REACT often provides food for POST 18, during field training exercises.

## Command Staff

A command staff is set up whenever a missing person is reported. The first deputy on the scene interviews all witnesses and makes the determination whether to call out search teams. The First Responder Team then receives a briefing and re-interviews the witnesses for basic information. This information usually includes: a detailed description of the missing person and his/her clothing, what equipment they might have, where they might have been heading, and other information as needed. Other information may include experience, length of time missing, knowledge of the area, general health, etc. Others on the command staff may include map readers and communication coordinators. The Command Staff is the people who set up the general plan of attack.

## Overhead Team

The next step is to set up an Overhead Team, which will be in charge of the search. The size of this team can be one to seven or eight people, depending on the mission. The most important person is the *Incident Commander* or Search Coordinator. This person is the overall leader. Their job is: to coordinate the activities of the searchers, overall planning, make search assignments, and to watch and evaluate search progress. Other key functions of the overhead team, which can be handled by the Incident Commander or others, include: logistics, operations and finances. *Logistics* is in charge of providing the coordinator with any necessary items, such as: fuel, communication, food, medical supplies, etc. *Operations* coordinates the search and decides which team searches where. *Finance* pays any bills and keeps the financial records.

Other personnel which are sometimes needed include: an *in-town coordinator*, an *advance base leader* and *team leaders*. The In-Town Coordinator keeps the overhead team supplied with help, food, helicopters, gas, search dogs, etc. The Advance Base Team Leader is in charge of a field base beyond the end-of-the-road base camp. Team Leaders are in charge of individual teams and report to the overhead team.

This Overhead Team decides what areas to search, what type of search to use and which teams are necessary.

## Base Camp

Base camp is the area where the search is planned and organized; it is also the place where all the important decisions are made. Base camp can consist of one truck at the side of a road to a parking lot or field filled with trucks, tents, campers and cars.

Present at base camp are a variety of people. Depending on the search, these can include: the overhead team, search units (resting or waiting for assignments), press (reporters and camera crews), friends and relatives of the missing person, and other members of the public. During a large search, the Incident Commander may assign others to help with "crowd control." This may include a liaison for the family, someone to give information and assignments to arriving search teams, a press officer (usually someone from the Sheriff's office), etcetera.

The family Liaison is in charge of helping the family. They will provide support and information about the progress of the search, make sure the family is provided with whatever they need (food, for example) and keep the press from bothering the family. Often, this liaison may just need to be someone for the family to talk to; answering questions about what is happening, gathering more information about the missing person or just letting the family members express their hopes and fears.

## Other possible base camp jobs

Another "job" may be coordination of arriving search teams. Each arriving team must be registered. The information collected may include: their radio call numbers, any special equipment they may have available and the names of every member of their team. Each team is then given the most current information on the missing person and assigned a search area.

The "press officer" is usually a member of the Sheriff's office. Their job is to give information to the press and keep them updated as new information comes in. This is an important job, as the press can be a hindrance, if they are allowed to bother the family or impede the searchers.

Often, untrained people will offer to help in the search. Although their offer is appreciated, they are usually discouraged from going out with the search teams for three reasons. First, they seldom have the proper training or equipment. They are emotionally attached to the missing person, which can impact their ability to think clearly and remain calm. They often do not understand that the team leaders are in charge of each team and resent being "told what to do" by teenagers. Lastly, with untrained searchers, there is a greater chance for mistakes. This may mean an area is not properly searched, or worse, another person may become lost.

## Types of Searches

Search and rescue groups are called out for a variety of reasons. These may include: ground searches for lost people; rescues of injured people; body recoveries; evidence searches; house-to-house searches and, occasionally, major disasters, such as fires, floods and major storms.

The main objective of any search is to find a missing person or object and make a safe rescue or recovery. Search teams from Post 18 are told, "Keep going in a straight line. If something is in your way, go under, over or through it."

There are three main types of ground searches:

**Type I** walking roads and trails, looking for clues or evidence.

**Type II** arm length — a closer group covering a field or streambed, for example.

**Type III** shoulder to shoulder this could be used for heavily wooded areas or evidence searches involving small objects (such as a bullet or weapon.)

The type of search is determined by a variety of factors. As the overhead team begins planning, maps of the search area are used to determine what specialized training or equipment may be needed. The type of terrain and weather conditions need to be taken into account in planning which search teams and what types of searches will be most effective.

# ABOUT THE AUTHOR

Kate McPhail loves writing for children and young teens. She is a retired teacher and enjoys spending time with her eleven grandchildren. She was a member of REACT for three years before joining Explorer Post 18 as an advisor to the Search and Rescue team. During her time in Search and Rescue, she was also an EMT 2, a volunteer 911 Operator and a Reserve Police Officer.

# Other books by Kate McPhail:

<u>No Escape!</u>   A woman wakes up in a mystery. She has to use her wits and bravery to figure out how to get away from an impossible and confusing situation. With no one to help her and with many twists and turns, this mystery will keep you guessing right up to the startling conclusion.

<u>Tale of Tails</u>   Beyond Mother Goose Books are stories, which use old familiar Nursery rhymes and give them an appealing twist! Tale of Tails is the first book in the set, which promises to become a favorite of children and adults everywhere. This delightful color book story tells "what really happened" to Little Bo-Peep's sheep! Children will love the story in which they will see some familiar characters. They will also enjoy coloring the delightful pictures, (drawn by <u>Larry Krackle</u>).

<u>The Money Tree</u>   The McPierson family had recently moved to Puyallup, Washington. Tom, aged ten, and his eight-year-old sister, Jamie, were excited to meet new friends. They soon formed a club--The West Main Five--and discovered the clue to a 25-year-old mystery! Using the library to research, they begin to put together an intriguing puzzle. Will the club solve the mystery that has baffled police for years? Who is the mysterious man who seems so interested in them? Where is the missing money?

<u>Rollin' Into Mystery</u> The West Main Five is back with a new mystery! They find a mysterious note; has someone been kidnapped? The Police have no reported kidnappings, just a missing person. Where is the mysterious Brad Parker? Why did he disappear from his job? Will the library have any clues to this new mystery?